Neelkamal:
The Bengali Batman

Raju Mahajan

This book was originally a thesis submitted to West Virginia State University in the fall of 2014 in partial fulfillment of the requirements for the degree of Master of Arts in Media Studies.

Cover Design by Moka

For Norah,
My loving daughter, my everything!

I sing this self-written Bengali lullaby for her:
Norah Moni
Shona Moni
Lokkhi Shona
Chader Kona
Jadur Kona

English Translation:
Norah Moni
[my] Piece of Jewel
[you are] A good kid
[my] Piece of the Moon
[my] Piece of Magic

Table of Contents

Foreword

I am so very honored to write the Foreword for Raju Mahajan's book, *Neelkamal: The Bengali Batman*. Originally, his thesis was titled "Deconstruction of a Bengali Batman." What an incredibly ambitious task to draw similarities between Bangladeshi and American superheroes, yet Mahajan fully succeeds. This book is a perfect example of how "deconstruction" can serve as a valuable rhetorical tool, one that uncovers shared paradigms of power between two very different cultures.

Mahajan first told me his idea to compare the American Batman to a Bengali folk hero when he was my graduate student at West Virginia State University in 2014. When he asked me to direct his thesis, I was quite thrilled. Here was a topic that was not only super interesting but also something that had never been done before.

Though, at the time, I knew nothing about Neelkamal, I realized instantly how unique and important this analysis would be. Certainly, Mahajan's book, based largely on his thesis, will add greatly to scholarly discussion. Not only is there no existing comparative analysis of Batman and Neelkamal, but there also, in fact, is very little comparative cultural research of any type between these two cultures.

Neelkamal: The Bengali Batman serves as a superb comparative cultural analysis between Eastern and Western supercharacters. Mahajan shows readers how, even though Neelkamal and Batman represent different cultures, genres and periods, they share many interesting similarities in their character, actions and goals. Mahajan highlights specific examples from their socioeconomic classes, accumulated wealth and levels of power, as well as their fighting techniques and their use of magical equipment. In addition, he touches on commonalities in their relationships and personal lives and their weak points and inner struggles.

Mahajan succeeds in showing how people living in different periods of history and different parts of the world still share a need for the same kind of superhero. What is most interesting, though, is not that each has superpowers beyond the common man but that these supercharacters also have the same kind of flaws, weaknesses and struggles in their personal lives. Mahajan succeeds in unrooting the oft-overlooked humanity shared by these two superheroes. Mahajan's discussion of how these superheroes were purposefully created to be less than perfect, much like regular humans, makes for a fascinating read.

Robin Broughton, Ph.D.

Preface

This book offers a unique comparative analysis that shows how different cultures and periods can share very similar paradigms of power. It serves as a comparative cultural analysis between the Eastern and Western supercharacters, Neelkamal and Batman. Though they represent different cultures, genres and periods, they share many interesting similarities in their character, actions and goals. There are similarities in their socioeconomic statuses of class, wealth and power; fighting techniques and magical equipment; relationships and personal lives; weaknesses and inner struggles; symbolic representations and archetypal images.

While there have been many studies conducted regarding American superheroes, there is neither any academic research on Bengali superheroes nor any comparative studies between a Bengali hero and a Western hero. Thus, the purpose of this research is to analyze an Eastern superhero with a Western theoretical scholarship. Using a comparative style of analysis makes this study interesting for both Western and Eastern audiences. This type of research is important to build a diversified, tolerant, liberal and peaceful international community. It will also create further opportunities for the development of joint media production and media analysis between these two cultures.

I did this research from 2011 to 2014 as part of my master's degree in media studies at West Virginia State University. After more than ten years, I still feel this is a great work. That's why I decided to make it a book: so that more people can read it and learn about the rich tradition of Bengali folklore. Bengali folklore is particularly rich in cultural elements, which makes it important to study for a better understanding of human civilization.

Raju Mahajan, Esq.
Bethesda, MD
08/23/2023

Acknowledgments

I thank Dr. Robin Broughton, Dr. Marc Porter and Dr. Tee Ford-Ahmed for their continuous guidance, encouragement and review of my research. I would not have been able to complete this work without their active engagement.

Introduction

Everyone likes supercharacters, from young children to adults and everyone in between. People connect to them because supercharacters teach morals, values and behaviors that are needed to change their readers and audiences into positive forces for society (Williams, 2011). At the very least, readers and audiences feel positive forces inside them when they read or watch any superhero's journey, whether they decide to act on those feelings or not.

Writer Mike Benton describes how a supercharacter appeals to people's fantasies of personal freedom, power and wins in the struggle of daily life, providing paragon characteristics of adolescent heroism (Benton, 1989). The United States provided a revolutionary advancement in the history of supercharacters during the Great Economic Depression of the 1930s. The post-Depression era took comic heroes into the zenith of popularity. Audience reception of the comic genre was so tremendous that the superheroes created in 1938 still dominate American culture today. Though other countries now have comic heroes like those created in America, they are still not as dominant as those in America. Superheroes of other cultures tend to appear as mythical heroes, folktale heroes, detective heroes or swashbuckler heroes.

This research presents us with an interesting comparative analysis between a modern comic hero and a traditional folktale hero. In particular, this intercultural analysis compares an American comic hero with a Bengali folktale hero by finding psychological similarities between the characters, actions and goals of Batman and Neelkamal. (See the Glossary for details about Bengali names and terms.) It also shows similarities in their historical, political, socio-economic and symbolic representations. This kind of intercultural analysis is rare between a Western and an Eastern superhero. As a result, this research will help broaden society's views on both Western and Eastern popular culture.

This type of research is also important for building a diversified, tolerant, liberal and peaceful international community. International understanding through cultural understanding is better known as Soft Power, Track Two Diplomacy or Citizen Diplomacy. Author Peng Er Lam acknowledges how Japan uses its cultural items like sushi, karaoke, J-pop, manga comics and anime cartoons to develop relations with the people of East Asia who are still struggling to overcome prejudices and challenges brought on during World War II.

Lam writes, "Japan is burnishing its international image through the popular medium of manga and anime. These cultural products appear to have the best of both worlds: distinctively Japanese in style and yet have universal appeal among the young" (2007). To that end, this analysis will create a new opportunity for the development of joint media production and media analysis between the United States and Bangladesh.

Fairytales or folktales have been a popular form of literature for children all over the world, although adults have been the primary audience of fairytales throughout history (Howson, 2007). Like myths, these stories were passed down through generations as an oral tradition before someone recorded them. Therefore, the messages that fairytales convey are always relatable to their current audience, regardless of time or place.

Although the basic structure and characteristics of these tales are universal and timeless, many cultural elements have been imposed on the story narratives with the long practice of oral storytelling. As a result, fairytales contain both universal human unconscious and representative cultural identities. Not only do fairytales provide entertainment for people of all ages, but they also essentially teach right from wrong and distinguish good from evil. In the post-9/11 age, characters and stories from folk resources are dominant in modern media storytelling (Stabile, 2009).

Joseph Campbell, in his seminal work *The Hero with a Thousand Faces*, cites many common patterns running through heroes' stories around the world, revealing that folk literature belonging to one culture usually has some similarities with another culture. It is also true that geographic, cultural, political, historical and social elements of a particular land enrich its folk literature (Shahed, 1993).

In the past, folk literature was passed from generation to generation without any intention of scientific preservation. Because of the nature of oral storytelling, folk literature contains very important elements for the exploration of the collective unconscious and hidden cultural treasures (Steele & Swinney 1978). Since these stories are a collective product of a culture, they contain the traditions, emotions, thoughts and values of their mother community. At the same time, since they were mostly oral, they relied on some human mnemonic devices and particular linguistic patterns that generations easily passed on over time (Ahmed 2006). Importantly, these linguistic devices not only impact the oral tradition of folklore but also its structure and story.

In Bengali culture, the earliest written format of folk material was primarily proverbs, and the oldest specimen of Bengali literature was *Charyapada* from the ninth century. This literature incorporated elements of Hindu mythology, Islamic history, Persian literature, Turkish literature and more (Ahmed 2006). The rich offerings of the Bengal Delta included folk songs, ballads, folktales, folk drama, rhymes, incantations, riddles and proverbs. This analysis focuses mostly on the folktales of Bengali literature.

Based on subject, meaning and form, Bengali folktales are classified into twelve groups (Ahmed 2006). There are fairytales, mythical tales, religious tales, adventure stories, heroic stories, sage tales, historical tales, legends, animal stories, fables and comic stories. Common plots are social issues like early marriages, polygamy, dowry, hatred between co-wives and stepmother envy. We also find some political elements in these stories like repression by the powerful, sufferings of the poor and weak, uneven distribution of wealth, racial discrimination and aristocracy. Though many spiritual elements are found within these stories, there is no mention of any religions, religious festivals or rituals. This absence of religion is very interesting in the context of this region since religion is one of the most significant social elements in the known history of the Indian subcontinent. Destiny and divinity play vital roles in the hero's journey in these stories.

However, Bengali folk literature did not get much attention until British rule in India. Following the European tradition of folktale collection and publication, many Bengali academicians and cultural representatives started to collect and publish different versions of Bengali folk literature from different regions.

In Europe, the tradition of collecting folklore gained new momentum when the German philologist Jakob Grimm and his brother Wilhelm published their seminal two-volume collection of German folktales titled *Kinder und Hausmiirchen* in 1812 (Shahed, 1993). This publication attracted the attention of researchers, academicians, liberators and nationalist leaders worldwide.

Within a very short period, many European countries published their own versions of oral stories, as did the colonial areas, including British India. Interestingly, the first few attempts to collect Indian folktales, including Bengalese folktales, were not made by natives but by colonial administrators, Anglican missionaries and travelers from Victorian England (Shahed, 1993). Missionaries William Morton and James Long published four compilations of Bengali Proverbs between 1832 and 1872. Sir George Griarson issued the first collection of Bengali folktales in 1873, followed by Reverend Lalbihary Dey in 1883 (Shahed, 1993).

Dakshinaranjan Mitra Majumder (1877-1957), one of the famous writers of Bengali children's literature, collected fairytales, hymns, ballads and humorous conversations and published them in four books. *Thakurmar Jhuli,* or *Grandmother's Tales*, published in 1909, was the first and most popular book. Rabindranath Tagore, the winner of the 1913 Nobel Prize in Literature, wrote the introduction of this anthology. Currently, this book is considered the icon of Bengali children's literature. Many characters from this book became so popular that they had strong influences in other media, such as children's theater, film, television dramas and comics. Sheyal Pondit (Fox the Professor),

Laalkamal-Neelkamal, Dalim Kumar and Byangoma-Byangomi (fictional birds) are some of the more popular characters. The superhero Neelkamal is from the folk story called *The Adventure of Laalkamal and Neelkamal*.

This research critically analyzes both the Batman and Neelkamal characters while simultaneously introducing Neelkamal to the modern Western world. There are interesting similarities between Batman and Neelkamal in their wealth and power, the magical equipment they use, their Oedipus complexes and personal lives, their weaknesses and inner struggles, and the symbolic representations of political history. Both characters experience the same kind of family tragedy during childhood that shapes their psychological development. Ultimately, both of them conquer their fears and establish themselves as symbols of justice by saving their people.

Chapter One

The Histories and Stories of Batman and Neelkamal

Batman is a comic book superhero co-created in 1939 by Bob Kane and Bill Finger. He is also known as the Caped Crusader, the Dark Knight, the World's Greatest Detective or, simply, the Bat. This character was brought to audiences by Detective Comics (DC), a company under Warner Brothers Entertainment.

Batman does not have any superpowers, rather, he makes use of his intellect, detective skills, science and technology, wealth, physical prowess and intimidation for his crime-fighting. Soon after his introduction, Batman became a popular character and gained his own comic book titled *Batman*, which eventually would turn out to be one of the most popular superhero characters in American history. The character adopted different elements and themes from various sources. Drawings of Leonardo da Vinci influenced the look and feel of Batman's costume. The persona of the 1919 fictional character Zorro and the style of 1930s horror films, especially for the movie *The Bat*, also influenced Batman's character.

In May 1939, Batman made his debut in DC #27, which was a six-page story. It turned out to be an immediate hit. In November 1939, the origin of Batman was fully fleshed out in DC #33. The story is about a boy, Bruce Wayne, the son of a wealthy philanthropist, Thomas Wayne. Thomas, his wife Martha and their 8-year-old son, Bruce, were coming out of a movie theater when a masked gunman, Joe Chill, came out of the shadows and asked for their wallets and jewelry. Chill first shot and killed Thomas and then did the same to Martha, who cried out for help right in front of their young boy. Bruce was traumatized at the sight of his parents' death. Afterward, Bruce was raised by his wise and loyal butler, Alfred Pennyworth, and inherited his family's vast fortune as well as his father's company, Wayne Enterprises. Standing before his parents' gravestones, Bruce made a solemn oath to avenge his dead parents.

At the age of fourteen, Bruce started a twelve-year adventure around the world to study and learn. For academics, he studied at Cambridge in England, the Sorbonne in France and other famous European universities. He also learned more practical skills. A Frenchman named Henri Ducard and an African bushman taught him about hunting, a ninja named Kirigi taught him about stealth, and several Nepalese monks taught him about healing.

The spring of 1940 also saw the first appearance of a supporting character for Batman, named Robin, in DC #38. This character lit up the series and added weight among the young readers. Batman is known to have more villains than any other superhero, and this informs one of the most popular and important pieces in Batman comics. Its first issue presented the most popular villains, the Joker and the Cat, who later became Catwoman. The year 1941 saw the introduction of the Penguin and, in 1942, Two-Face appeared to steal the scene.

In 1943, Batman appeared on the silver screen as a 15-part serial, *Batman*, and emerged on radio in the late 1940s. On January 12, 1966, Batman started appearing on television. The 1970s saw a decline in comic book sales, and Batman disappeared from television as well. In 1986, writer-artist Frank Miller created a limited miniseries titled *Batman: The Dark Knight Returns*, which yet again increased Batman's popularity. The 1989 hit movie *Batman*, directed by Tim Burton, further reignited interest in the character. In 1992, *Batman: The Animated Series* debuted on television.

In 1993, Batman appeared in the film *Batman: Mask of the Phantasm*, followed by *The New Batman Adventures*, *Batman Beyond*, and *Justice League*. In 2005, 2008 and 2012, director Christopher Nolan came out with a Batman trilogy—*Batman Begins*, *The Dark Knight* and

The Dark Knight Rises, respectively. This trilogy was not only highly profitable but was also critically acclaimed. Nolan's casting of Christian Bale as Bruce Wayne and Heath Ledger as the Joker attracted both critical and popular attention.

Neelkamal's history comes from the Bengali folk story called *The Adventure of Neelkamal and Laalkamal*. (See Appendix B for an edited version of the original translation.) Neelkamal (Neel) and Laalkamal (Laal) are half-brothers. Their father is a king. Laalkamal is the son of the king and the older queen, and Neelkamal is the son of the king and the younger queen. This younger queen is a demon in the disguise of a very beautiful woman. Thus, Neel is a half-human, half-demon. Laal and Neel's birth names are Prince Kushum and Prince Ajit, respectively. Though the demon queen does not like it, Prince Ajit's best friend is his half-brother, Prince Kushum.

The demon queen first came to this kingdom to take control of the political power. Eventually, she kills the human queen, invites thousands of demons from her own country into this kingdom, curses Kushum and Ajit into the forms of a gold ball and an iron ball and then buries them in a bamboo bush far away from the capital. Later, the two princes reincarnate from balls-turned-into-eggs as the mighty fighters, Neelkamal and Laalkamal. The two brothers then go to another kingdom, which is also suffering from demons, and eradicate the demons of that land. They then marry the two beautiful princesses who are the daughters of that king.

Hearing this story, the demon queen (the mother of Neel) sends a messenger to the princes to convey that their father is very sick and that only a special oil can save his life. That oil can be found only in the demon queen's hair. The demon queen devised this plot in hopes that the demons would kill the Kamal brothers during their attempt to save their father. However, Neelkamal and Laalkamal have an incredible amount of wit and muscle. They first destroy the kingdom of demons, kill Neel's grandmother and finally kill the queen mother, thus saving the whole earth from all of the alien monsters.

Chapter Two

Wealth and Power

M ission convention is essential to the superhero character because someone who doesn't act selflessly to aid others in time of need is not heroic and, therefore, not a hero (Coogan, 2006). Mighty but selfless is the key to the superhero character. He can be wealthy or poor, but he must be powerful and selfless. From the son of a billionaire to the son of a prostitute, superheroes are from all socioeconomic classes.

Batman is an American billionaire, playboy, industrialist and philanthropist. Neelkamal is a prince of a wealthy king and later marries the princess daughter of another wealthy king. Both individuals are very rich, as it seems that many fictional superheroes are. It is easy for the audience to draw a legitimate relationship between wealth, power and heroism.

Human cognitive psychology has its own preconception of a hero as wealthy and powerful. This preconception helps wealthy superheroes win public support easily. An audience will not accept a powerless man as a hero. People do not want to compromise their dream character. Our concept of a protector is probably that we are poor but he is rich, we are weak but he is strong, we are incomplete but he is complete. It is very rational for the audience to imagine a wealthy superhero who ignores his self-interest and works for the good of humankind by using his power.

Democracy is the first political system that created an opportunity for the people to rise to the peak of power. All prior political, social and economic systems were dominated by elites. Interestingly, political leaders failed to gain the position of superhero. The reason behind this is that they are only in power for a certain time, and that they are dependent on executive, legislative, judiciary and other branches for decision-making and implementation.

That is why the superhero of Gotham City is not the Mayor, but Batman, who is not legitimized to exercise power. People's demand for a supercharacter is that they are to be independent, self-sufficient and neutral. Even in the 2008 Batman film *The Dark Knight*, directed by Christopher Nolan, Harvey Dent, the District Attorney of Gotham City, admits the failure of democracy. He references Greek mythology and says, "When their enemies were at the gates, the Romans would suspend democracy and appoint one man to protect the city." Batman and Neelkamal represent that "one man."

Superheroes must need to feel a fatherly dedication to the people. Dedication inspires him to protect people. Bruce Wayne is the prince of Gotham (*Batman Begins*, 2005). Neelkamal is a prince, too. This indicates that the nature of a superhero's power is absolute, not democratic.

The word "superpower" indicates something above human power. Political power is the accumulated power of individual citizens. Thus, superheroes cannot be community members but have to be "others." Bruce Wayne cannot fight crime as Bruce himself, so he needs a disguise. Neelkamal is a prince who is half-demon, so there already is a clear difference between him and his masses. This disguise or difference helps each individual become a hero from the very beginning. Otherwise, they would need to fight with other community members to gain leadership, which costs valuable time and power.

Chapter Three

Magical Equipment

While Batman uses a large arsenal of specialized bat-motif gadgets in his crime-fighting, Neelkamal only uses a sword. But a very significant and symbolic similarity between them is their relationship with birds. Both of them have very close ties with birds in their war against crime. The "batsuit," especially the cape, helps Batman fly from one roof to another, and Byangoma-Byangami, a fictional bird, helps Neelkamal fly to the demons' land. This fictional use of birds as a means of transportation is very popular in almost all mythology.

The bird is a symbol of the spirit or soul. In Latin, "aves" meant both "birds" and "ancestral spirits," or ghosts or angels. Many Indo-European mythology and fairytales tell us that souls could take the form of birds after death (Walker, 1983). Thus, they divided birds into good and bad, similar to heaven and hell. Many scientists and science fiction writers were also inspired by the bird. For instance, Leonardo da Vinci was fascinated by the phenomenon of flight. He studied the flight mechanics of birds and finally came up with a basic idea of a flying machine, which is close to the present-day helicopter. The history of humans' desire for flight inspired by the bird is very old and scientific.

Birds had a significant role in Bruce Wayne's inner transformation into Batman and Ajit's reincarnation as Neelkamal, not just as a mode of transportation. During his childhood, when Bruce Wayne fell into an underground cave, he was scared by a large swarm of bats, and later, while in his father's study, a large bat came crashing into him. Bruce saw this as a dark omen and recalled his fear of bats as a child, deciding to use the bat as his symbol. It was then that the true idea of Batman formed in Bruce's mind. He later transformed his fear into strength when he returned to the same cave with thousands of bats.

Similarly, the demon queen cursed Ajit and Kushum into the forms of gold and iron balls and buried them in a bamboo bush. A farmer later found those balls-turned-into-eggs in a bamboo stem but threw them away, because he was afraid that they were snake eggs. Ajit and Kushum then reincarnated from those blue and golden eggs. Since an egg is typically an organic vessel in which birds' embryos first begin to develop until birth, Neelkamal is a symbolic son of a bird.

The superhero's goal is not the main justification for his or her adventure. Journeys of supercharacters are more focused on the freedom of the masses than exhibiting his or her own superpower. As birds are a symbol of freedom and independence, they best symbolize superheroes as opposed to a ferocious animal like the tiger or lion. That is why we don't have any "Tigerman" or "Lionman." Since flying birds cannot rest in the sky, they are the symbol of a restless journey. This restless journey reflects the nature of crime-fighting for Batman and Neelkamal.

Another common fictional mode of air transportation is the cloud. Neelkamal's mother, the demon queen, has the magical power to ride on clouds. Cloud seeding, or creating an artificial cloud, is now used for many purposes all over the world. Hopefully, a future Batman supervillain will be able to create clouds from a sophisticated machine and use them to escape from the police. One could picture this taking place in a movie about Neelkamal, too.

Chapter Four

Women, Loves and Personal Lives

Both Batman and Neelkamal are the perfect examples of the Byronic romantic hero when considering their personal lives and loves. Over the years, through comics, television shows and movies, Batman has had different loves. However, the one factor that has remained the same is that Bruce Wayne can never have a lasting relationship. Ultimately, he is forced to choose between his life as Batman and his personal life, and every time, he chooses to be Batman.

Bruce Wayne is not a real playboy, but he has always pretended to be one to conceal his secret identity as Batman. The people of Gotham City view Bruce Wayne as a rich philanthropist who does nothing but fly around to exotic locations with many beautiful women. They do not suspect him of being the kind of man who dresses up in a bat costume and risks his life to fight crime, either willingly or unwillingly, to protect Gotham.

We see this relationship crisis in Christopher Nolan's Batman trilogy. Rachel Dawes and Bruce Wayne are childhood friends, and they love each other. However, Bruce's duty as Batman gets in the way of their relationship. In the 2005 movie *Batman Begins,* Rachel tells him that they cannot be together as long as he is Batman, because a true relationship takes a level of dedication that Bruce cannot give her. In the 2008 movie *The Dark Knight*, Bruce Wayne is ready to retire from being Batman and rekindle his love with Rachel, but she has a new love interest named Harvey who has the time to dedicate to her. Rachel finds that she must choose between a man who can give her the attention and stability she needs or her childhood friend whose "career" is too demanding for him and will keep him away from her. In the end, like in a Greek tragedy, neither Harvey nor Batman can have Rachel after the Joker arranges her death.

Since Bruce Wayne lost his mother during his childhood, has no sister and spent his youth learning martial arts and other fighting tactics in some very remote mountainous region, he has an intuitive desire and long-building thirst for love. This thirstiness is clear in his lifestyle, especially in Nolan's version of Batman. We find that the basic theme of the Batman mythos is that Bruce Wayne can never have a lasting relationship. In every story, he must always choose his duty as Batman over his personal happiness.

Similarly, since his mother was a demon and tried to kill him, Neel did not know what a mother's love was. Though he married Princess Elaboti, he left for the demon's kingdom to kill the demon queen, his own maternal grandmother. Finally, what is called a "happy ending" occurs when Neelkamal kills his own mother. Throughout his crime-fighting, Neelkamal fights with female characters who would typically be expected to love him. When the story ends, all the demons are dead and Earth is safer, but Neelkamal is the only representative of the previous demons. As half-human and half-demon, he is nothing more than a lone knight left to protect the earth like Bruce Wayne.

Gotham City's landscape and architecture is very beautiful. Its rich economy makes it attractive to all, but the citizens are always afraid of terrorism. Unlimited and unique terrorists threaten the city routinely. Since the government has failed to protect the people of Gotham, they must rely on a protector over whom they have no control. In fact, Batman is an antihero. The entire situation has made Gotham City a haven full of evil things. This duality is the physical manifestation of Bruce Wayne's life. The murder of his parents during his childhood, the refusal from his beloved and his identity conflict are an exploration of romanticism in the world of the public protector who failed to protect his personal life. He is an unhappy man who hides his sorrow in the veil of a playboy image.

Neelkamal's kingdom is also very similar to Bruce Wayne's Gotham City. His father is a powerless, weak king. Demons massacred the kingdom and hopeless citizens left the country. His elder brother is not strong enough to fight alone against demons. He is the only hope to save the Earth from destruction and bring citizens back into the kingdom. He also needs to clear his position concerning humans since he has blood relations with the demons.

The blue flower symbolizes both the lives of Batman and Neelkamal. This blossom is a symbol of inspiration, desire, love and an infinite journey. It gives a cooling antidote to its receiver, and its giver represents mystic faithfulness and loyalty. The blue flower is referenced in the film *Batman Begins*. The name "Neelkamal" originally came from two parts— "neel" and "kamal," which in English means exactly "blue" and "flower."

Chapter Five

Weaknesses

U nlike other superheroes, Batman has no special power as an ordinary human. That is why he does not have any special weaknesses, like Superman's kryptonite. Batman's weaknesses are similar to other human limitations. He is vulnerable to bullets, fire and more. His enemies know his weaknesses and also think that he is especially weak because of his reluctance to take human life.

Neelkamal is also a mortal being like Batman. In fact, he went through the reincarnation process in his story. During the very first important demon-fighting night, he even fell asleep due to the very human feeling of being tired.

Superheroes' weaknesses are not essential for the hero himself but rather for the audience and storyteller. If the main character has no weakness, then the story will be flat and boring. Suspense is the key element for superhero stories, which comes from weakness. The desires of an audience to get a specific result from the story and their intention to intervene in the events of the storyline create suspense for each member. This desire is then frustrated by the inability of the viewer to express the information that they lack to the character. The audience only feels compelled to intervene in the story when the main character's strength or weakness is very similar to the one in his or her personal life. Since Batman is a human, and his strengths and weaknesses are very human, the audience can easily relate to him. If superheroes do not have weaknesses, then what is the struggle?

Superheroes' weaknesses are also very important for storytellers, writers and directors. Since the weaknesses of main characters play a vital role in creating plots of dramatic narrative—including exposition, rising action, climax, falling action and revelation or catastrophe—then writers or directors can easily intervene in the story, creating weakness and driving it in a different direction based on his or her creativity. The craft of storytelling and creating charismatic characters are two vital components behind every successful story.

Weakness made Batman more popular than any other American superhero. It provided the opportunity to create some tremendous supervillains, which made the Batman series a must-read for enthusiastic readers. Similarly, on his first demon-fighting night, when the demons were late, Neelkamal fell asleep, allowing the demons to attack and attempt to eat Laalkamal. When this chaos broke Neelkamal's sleep, he then fought the demons, killed all of them and saved Laalkamal. This story tells us how poorly Laalkamal, the elder son of the king, did in fighting demons and how important Neelkamal's role was in saving the world.

Chapter Six

Inner Struggles

In Batman mythology, there are two parallel struggles. Batman's first struggle is to protect Gotham City from criminals and corrupt officials while restoring the hope of the mass people, which is very important for the city's survival. Since it is one of the richest cities in the world, criminals are everywhere. Betrayal of cops and officials is frequent because of the unlimited supply of money. Therefore, Gotham needs someone like Batman for its survival.

However, Bruce Wayne's personal struggle is to survive in this cruel world where his parents were shot dead in front of him. Gotham failed to protect them, and it was very hard to survive as an orphan. Again, he is determined to avenge his parents' deaths. Being the "Prince of Gotham," he knows that he will never understand the world because he has never experienced life outside of Gotham City. As a result, Bruce decides to travel the world for several years.

After learning various ways to fight the criminal underworld, he transforms himself into a revengeful angel who is strong enough to protect himself first. He also needs to follow the law, however, and be obedient just as his father was. All of these conflicting emotional factors make his transformation very critical. He has to sacrifice his very human desire for love and emotion for his noble job.

Bruce's survival is dependent on Gotham's survival, and Gotham is dependent on Batman. Therefore, Batman will not survive if Bruce cannot sacrifice his personal life. There is a critical survival triangle between Bruce Wayne, Gotham City and Batman.

Similarly, there are two parallel struggles in *The Adventure of Neelkamal and Laalkamal*. While Neel's outer struggle of fighting demons and saving the world is comparatively straightforward, his inner struggle is more complex, like Bruce's. In his previous life as Prince Ajit, he always kept a distance from his demon mother and had a very friendly relationship with his half-brother, Prince Kushum. Naturally, his mother was not happy about his friendship with her stepson and archenemy.

Understanding his mother's evil intention, he advises Prince Kushum to also keep a distance from her. So, there is a psychological conflict between mother and son. His mother later turns them into balls with her magical power and buries them, which is the death of innocent Ajit and Kushum. After the reincarnation of Neelkamal as a strong fighter, he finds that his own mother is his archenemy.

Like Bruce Wayne, Neel's motivations for fighting evil are the death of his kind and honest stepmother, the helpless situation of his father the king, and the murder of himself and his brother in their previous lives. Just after his reincarnation, Neel also leaves his country, like Bruce, to fight with a lesser species of demons, the Khokkosh. This time of fighting the Khokkosh helps him get ready for his ultimate adventure and gets rid of his weakness.

We can compare Neel's first Khokkosh-fighting with Bruce's traveling to different parts of the world, learning crime-fighting and transforming his fear into strength along the way. In Neel's final adventure in the demons' kingdom, he uses his identity as the grandson of the queen of the demon's land to gain the advantage in crime-fighting, which is similar to Batman's frequent use of Bruce's playboy image or billionaire reputation. Neelkamal's first inner struggle is to overcome his identity as a demon to address the fight of good against evil. His second inner struggle is to recapture his identity as a demon to make his outer struggle easier.

Chapter Seven

Symbolic Representations

A lmost all superhero characters represent a certain period and place. Though Gotham City is in the northern part of the United States, it represents the whole country. Gotham City's developed economy and unlimited criminal supply are indicative of the post-Depression economic growth and political culture of the United States from the 1940s to the 1970s. We can find a shadow of former U.S. President John F. Kennedy in Bruce Wayne until the 1970s. Like Kennedy, Bruce is from a famous family, travels to many countries, studies in famous universities and is a playboy with strong political views.

However, Christopher Nolan mentions in a documentary by *The History Channel* that he adopted many ideas from another U.S. President, Theodore Roosevelt, and his father "Thee" Roosevelt, to create the characters of Bruce Wayne and his father Thomas (*Batman Unmasked*, 2008). Throughout the 1980s and into later decades, Batman becomes darker and more of an anti-hero. The villains also become psychologically more complex, which represents Cold War and post-Cold War political complexity. The most recent Batman trilogy, directed by Christopher Nolan, is influenced by the ongoing war against terrorism. Villains like Bane, the Joker and Ra's al Ghul remind us of extremist militants. Conflicts over nuclear weapons in the 2012 movie *The Dark Knight Rises* represent one of the main tensions of the twenty-first century.

Similarly, the demons' control over Neelkamal's kingdom represents foreign aggression in Bengal from the 13th century to the 18th century.

The demon queen is the symbol of their institutional acceptance and rehabilitation in the political process. Many of them settled in Bengal permanently and became Bengali, which made the people a homogenous but considerably diverse ethnic group with heterogeneous origins. They are Neelkamals. The weak king is the symbol of Bengal's political leaders who failed to protect the country throughout history. Neelkamal is the symbol of a new generation who has blood from diverse ethnicities in its veins but fights and wins victory over colonists.

Superhero characters always proportionally reflect modern times and follow the changing views of the audience within their own culture. For example, the next Batman could be a college dropout billionaire like Bill Gates or Steve Jobs, who are the real-life heroes of this era.

Chapter Eight

Archetypal Similarities

Carl Jung defined how we infer universal understanding from specific symbols, peoples, terms, processes or specific objects in the world around us. He outlined five main archetype categories to framework his concept of the collective unconscious—the Self, the Shadow, the Anima, the Animus and the Persona. All of these archetypes are present in Christopher Nolan's *Batman Begins* and in the tale of Neelkamal, thus influencing the storylines in both cases.

The Shadow

The repressed thoughts and emotions that live within our subconscious are the Shadow. These are the traits, fears and thoughts that we often hide from others and even ourselves—our dark side.

In his childhood, while playing in the family's garden, Bruce Wayne falls down a hidden well. He is injured and scared by the thousands of bats that he faces in the well. He was never able to forget that nightmare, and it was always fresh in his mind. Those bats are Bruce's external tormentors that confirm the Shadow archetype.

Similarly, during the young prince's childhood, the demon queen was very hostile to her stepson, Laalkamal. Neelkamal knew this and advised his half-brother to keep a distance from his mother. He knew that his mother was an evil person who always wished to harm his beloved brother. One night while the two princes were sleeping, a giant demon attacked both of them. They managed to survive, but the demon queen cursed them into the shapes of an iron ball and a gold ball. This shocking childhood memory shaped Neel's psyche permanently and inspired him to fight against his mother. This fear is the Shadow.

The Self

The Self is the unique identity of a person. It contains an individual's conscious and unconscious thoughts. These conscious and unconscious thoughts are what separate a person from the surrounding environment. It helps a hero to discover who he or she is.

Bruce Wayne's entire childhood and youth helped him to find his true Self. The death of his parents, training under the League of Shadows, failure of revenge, Rachel's presence, and connecting with poor and weak people helped him discover that he is a lonely crime fighter. This identification is the key point of the Batman mythology.

Similarly, the process of facing hostility from his mother, turning into an egg and undergoing reincarnation into a mighty prince helped Neelkamal find his Self as well.

The Anima and the Animus

The Anima represents the female aspect of the male psyche, and the Animus represents the male aspect of the female psyche. We connect with the collective unconscious through our Anima or Animus.

Rachel Dawes is Bruce's Anima. She completes her quest for revenge by educating him that true law and justice can result in a just society, but that violent revenge cannot. On the other hand, there is no important female character or love interest for Neelkamal. His wife does not have any role in the crime-fighting. However, this lack of Anima also portrays the best presence of the entire Anima.

The Persona

The Persona is our mask, or what we allow the world to see and understand about ourselves. It protects our ego from unwanted events around us. Bruce's Persona is a billionaire playboy or caped crusader. As for Neelkamal, his Persona is half-monster or mighty prince, which hides his human desire for a mother's love and ordinary family ties.

Conclusion

Batman and Neelkamal both have unusual childhoods. Violence and bloodshed shape their psychological development at an early age. These traumatic memories keep them away from their regular personal lives and inspire them to be crime-fighting vigilantes. They are victims of tragedy but also symbols of hope and justice. They go through a metamorphosis period to change themselves from the victim to the savior. They are afraid at first, but then they overcome their own fears and establish justice. Both of them suffer from guilt and take on the responsibility of a crusader to heal their own sufferings. They are rich, strong and powerful. Their power is absolute and independent. They use their power and intelligence as weapons against evil. Both of them have their own sidekick to help them—Robin for Batman and Laal for Neel.

Birds impact the reincarnation process of Bruce and Neel psychically and symbolically. Their restless duty to save their world is similar to a bird's restless flying in the sky. Bruce Wayne's relationship with Rachel swings back and forth between girlfriend and mother archetypes. Neel kills his own mother, his archenemy. Both of these are different dimensions of an Oedipus complex. This complex helps us understand their motif of crime fighting. Both of them share the same kind of inner struggle and identity conflict between ego and alter ego. Since both men have two different Personas, and one Persona influences and counters the other significantly, their inner conflicts are more severe than the outer conflicts with villains.

Batman and Neelkamal are Byronic heroes—proud and moody, cynical and implacable in revenge and yet capable of deep and strong affection. Both Gotham City and Neel's country are presented in their stories in such a way that we can call them heavens full of evil forces. Though they have rich economies and developed infrastructures, they also have male-dominated patriarchal societies, weak political institutions, leadership crises, irresponsible citizens and mass corruption.

Batman mythology represents the post-Depression period to present-day events in America, while Neelkamal and other Bengal heroes represent colonial occupations and their institutionalization of Bengal since the thirteenth century.

Appendix A

Methodology and Literature Review

This book is mainly a deconstruction of two heroes from two different cultures. According to deconstructionist critics, language is not a stable entity, especially in written format, and we can never exactly say what we mean. Therefore, any single piece of information can carry many different values depending on time, space, reader, mode, environment and many other variables. In fact, any single piece of information can carry multiple meanings in the same situation because language itself is ambiguous (Balkin, 1996).

Jacques Derrida, along with other philosophers and critics, developed the concept of deconstruction as a series of techniques for reading texts. Therefore, Derrida called it an activity of reading and not a method (Balkin, 1996). However, because of its popularity, this technique is often used as a synonym for criticizing or analyzing in many academic fields including law, literature, philosophy, art and anthropology. Many deconstructive arguments rotate around the analysis of conceptual binary oppositions.

One of these famous oppositions is between speech and writing (Derrida, 1976). Any deconstructive critic tries to find out the privileged one in every opposition couple. One term may be privileged because someone considers it to be primary, natural or general, while the other is viewed as secondary, artificial, peripheral or derivative. However, this comparative conception of status is very subjective and situational. Moreover, since something can have more than one opposite, many different types of privileging can occur simultaneously. We can analyze privileging between two particular opposite objects in several ways.

For instance, throughout this analysis, the reader can find privileging between hero and non-hero. The focus of this thesis is the deconstruction of the comparative status between the binary opposition of a hero and a common person. Our heroes and villains are the symbolic representation of ourselves—both as groups and as individuals. By this representation or process of identity construction, these hero images tell us who we are and what we stand for. Conversely, villain images give us a sense of who we are not and of what we stand against (Thomson, 2005).

Considering these functional definitions of hero and villain, we can judge our real-world societies. Since we find more villains than heroes in the real world society, society defines itself negatively in terms of "what it is not" and "which it stands against" instead of "what it is" and "what it stands for." Thus, societies become ever emptier and more hostile (Thomson, 2005).

Therefore, we need influential fictional hero characters to keep the high moral standards of the people. German philosopher Martin Heidegger said that the chosen hero of the group works like a mirror, reflecting an idealized image of the group itself. Chosen heroes focus our common sense on what is most important in our lives, shaping our ideas about which battle we should fight, as well as how we should go about fighting it.

Certainly, superheroes are cultural icons. Fictional comic superheroes have been very popular since the 1940s, but their presence in almost every form of media and their recent success in the entertainment business have attracted extra attention (Postrel, 2006). Canadian superhero Captain Chanuck, for instance, could be an ideal representative of Canadian culture. He is now more than a comic book relic since he is a key item in the construction of modern Canadian cultural identity and consciousness (Edwardson, 2003, p. 184). Similarly, Captain Ultra of Japan, the Great Ten of China, the Bogatyri of Russia, and the 99 of the Middle East are examples of superheroes all over the world.

Bengal (Bangladesh and West Bengal of India) also has its own group of superheroes, but most of them are mythological or folktale heroes. There are no mentionable re-creations of them in modern and new media. For instance, Neel, a fairytale character, is very popular in Bengal. He has a notable presence in children's literature, music, theater and local comics. However, there are no films, mainstream television series or video games based on Neelkamal's adventure. Batman, on the other hand, with roots similar to that of Odysseus from Greek mythology, has been re-envisioned in several multimedia outlets like comics, television, games and films. Batman's presence in all these media types for more than seven decades with newer and newer storytelling and retelling developed into a modern mythology of Batman (Plouffe, 2000).

Over the last 20 years, comic book characters have become stars all over the world with their glamour and audience appeal (Postrel, 2006). We have some clear examples of how these characters have shaped and influenced other cultures in intercultural studies (Bhatia, 2006). They are good subjects for intercultural studies because academic articles comparing two superheroes from two different cultures are very rare. This literature review uses superheroes as cultural representatives in an intercultural study.

Carl Jung wrote about the fundamental similarities among images that evoke strong emotions in people. Jung called them archetypal images. He explained them as an expression of the collective unconscious. We also find archetypal images in Bengal folktale stories. The pattern of narrative in *The Adventure of Neelkamal and Laalkamal* also displays a similar structure and storytelling to Batman and many other European fairytales. Jung and many others described this pattern as the archetypal journey of the hero. Jung says in a brief definition of the collective unconscious (1981):

> "[A] more or less superficial layer of the unconscious is undoubtedly personal. I call it the personal unconscious. But this personal unconscious rests upon a deeper layer, which does not derive from personal experience and is not

a personal acquisition but is inborn. This deeper layer I call the collective unconscious. I have chosen the term 'collective' because this part of the unconscious is not individual but universal; in contrast to the personal psyche, it has contents and modes of behavior that are more or less the same everywhere and in all individuals. It is, in other words, identical in all men and thus constitutes a common psychic substrate of a suprapersonal nature, which is present in every one of us."

Again, he defines collective unconsciousness in another volume as having "contents which do not originate in personal acquisitions, but in the inherited possibility of psychic functioning in general" (Jung 8, pp. 485). The contents of the collective unconscious are archetypes. In more than one place, Jung emphasizes that (1981):

"It was manifestly not a question of inherited ideas but of an inborn disposition to produce parallel thought-formations, or rather of identical psychic structures common to all men, which I later called the archetypes of the collective unconscious. It is not a question of a specifically racial heredity, but of a universally human characteristic nor is it a question of inherited ideas, but of a functional disposition to produce the same, or very similar ideas."

Although the backgrounds of Batman and Neelkamal include different cultures, geographic locations, genres and times, this research finds many interesting common cultural phenomena in their characters, struggles and goals. It finds similarity in the archetypal journey of the hero or archetypal image, which is an expression of the universal collective unconscious. These archetypal images are not just personal unconscious; Jung calls them "collective" because they come from a deeper layer of the psyche and are present in every hero. This Jungian concept of archetype is very similar to Campbell's idea of the monomyth, or the hero's journey. Campbell defines a hero's journey as the following (1968):

> "A hero ventures forth from the world of common day into a region of supernatural wonder: fabulous forces are there encountered, and a decisive victory is won: the hero comes back from this mysterious adventure with the power to bestow boons on his fellow man."

However, scholars question the very validity of Campbell's monomyth and universal hero's journey. For instance, Donald J. Cosentino remarks, "It is as important to stress differences as similarities" (Cosentino, 1998). Marta Weigle rejects the monomyth from a feminist perspective. The research conducted in this book seeks to critically consider both the similarities and differences across the narrative and then work to deconstruct each.

Appendix B

The Adventure of Neelkamal and Laalkamal

Adapted from *The Original Bengali Book of Fairytales*
Thakumar Jhuli by Dakshinaranjan Mitra Majumdar

A long, long time ago, there was a king and his two queens. The first queen was a human and she had a son named Kushum. The other queen was a demon, which no one in the kingdom was aware of, and she had a son whose name was Ajit.

The two princes, Kushum and Ajit, were very friendly with one another and loved each other deeply. When the demon queen saw how much the two boys loved each other, it filled her with hatred toward Kushum to the point that she longed for an opportunity to kill him and eat his flesh. Since her own son, Ajit, was Kushum's constant companion, the demon queen was unable to do anything against Kushum.

Then the demon queen decided to try a different tactic. She used her evil magical powers to infect the human queen with an incurable disease that caused her to become very ill and die. The king and the whole kingdom sank into deep sorrow as they mourned the death of their beautiful and pure human queen!

Soon afterward, Ajit came to realize that his evil demon queen mother was behind the terrible event. Feeling protective over his half-brother, Kushum, Ajit did his best to comfort him and keep him safe from the evil queen. The demon queen, however, became furious when she saw how her son was carefully protecting Kushum. As a result, she cast her evil spell throughout the whole kingdom and caused the death of all the royal elephants and horses in the whole region.

One night when the two princes were fast asleep, the evil demon queen summoned a demon companion, Rakkhosh, into the Kingdom and ordered him to kill Kushum. The demon obeyed, picking up Kushum and beginning to take his life from him.

At that moment, the king suddenly entered the room and saw that a big, horrible demon was holding his son and trying to kill him! Immediately drawing his royal sword, the king rushed forward, but the demon queen quickly stepped out of the shadows and paralyzed the king by releasing powers from her magical hair.

The poor king was now completely paralyzed and watched helplessly as the horrible evil demon killed his beloved son, Kushum, and consumed his flesh. Feeling intense pain and sorrow because he was unable to do anything to save his son, the king's eyes flooded with tears at the terrible sight. Meanwhile, the wicked demon queen cackled with delight because her evil wish was finally fulfilled.

At that moment, Ajit awoke from his sleep to find that his beloved elder brother, Kushum, had been cruelly murdered and devoured by an evil demon, right in front of his paralyzed father the king and his evil mother the demon queen! Filled with rage and intense agony, Ajit rose and attacked the demon with a vicious blow to its head. The Rakkhosh fell to the ground with a loud cry and painfully heaved up a large golden egg onto the floor before fleeing from the room.

Seeing all this take place, the demon queen was filled with fury. She stepped forward and struck her son so hard that he fell to the floor, lifeless. Seeing that Ajit was dead, the wretched mother consumed her own son's flesh, but when she was finished, she vomited a large iron egg from her mouth.

With both princes Kushum and Ajit now dead, the evil demon queen took the golden and iron eggs to the roof of the king's palace. There, a whole gathering of flesh-eating demons had arrived in preparation to go throughout the whole land and destroy the people. Seeing all of them, the queen announced, "O demon friends, go kill and devour the humans!

After eating their flesh, return to the land of the demons and I shall remain to rule this country in the presence of the paralyzed king!"

The demons obeyed, going throughout the kingdom and destroying the lives of one thousand countrymen before leaving the region and returning to their own land. As she watched from the roof of the king's palace, the evil demon queen felt satisfied, so she went down and buried the golden and iron eggs in a bamboo garden beside the Holy River.

The next day, the kingdom was a terrible sight with dead bodies and skeletons scattered throughout the land and heaps of human corpses found in every street. Meanwhile, all of the remaining people had already fled the country, leaving as soon as they heard the news that evil demons devoured their beloved princes, Kushum and Ajit, and paralyzed their good king.

***

Several days later, a farmer was working in the bamboo garden when he came upon a great tree. The fresh air from the river swirled around the bamboo tree just as the farmer began to cut into it. Suddenly, two giant eggs fell from the stalk of the bamboo tree! The farmer looked on in amazement as the two eggs—one blue and one red—began to hatch, revealing two beautiful royal figures—the Blue Prince and the Red Prince. Dressed all in royal attire, the two princes adjusted their crowns and their swords as they prepared to depart on a mission.

The farmer, seeing this astonishing sight take place in front of him, felt overwhelmed and fell to the ground, unconscious. When he finally recovered consciousness, he found that the remaining pieces of eggs were transformed—the blue eggshells turned into iron and the red eggshells became gold. Feeling glad, the farmer rose and began to make a sickle out of the iron pieces. Then, he took the gold and made some beautiful jewelry for his wife.

Meanwhile, the Red Prince and the Blue Prince were traveling far away throughout the country. Of course, these two were none other than the reincarnated forms of princes Kushum and Ajit, now known by two new names—Laalkamal and Neelkamal.

***

After a long journey, the two princes arrived in a country where many small demons called Khokkosh lived among the people. Every day, the demons devoured a whole family in the village, which caused great fear throughout the region. The king of this place declared that if any powerful princes were able to destroy the Khokkosh, they would be given rule over the country and receive his two beloved and beautiful daughters in marriage.

When the two princes arrived and heard about the declaration, they appeared before the king and requested his permission to kill all the Khokkosh in the country. The king agreed to allow the two powerful young men to try, but he warned both Laalkamal and Neelkamal that all the other attempts by others had been in vain. Not about to give up, the two princes decided to wait out in a secluded room in the palace where the Khokkosh were reported to have attacked the night before with their swords.

Laalkamal and Neelkamal waited for hours until it grew close to midnight, but no demons had shown up. As the princes' eyes started to become heavy, Neelkamal told Laalkamal that he was going to rest for a while, but told Laalkamal that if any Khokkosh arrived, to always say the name of Neelkamal first before saying the name of Laalkamal.

Shortly after midnight, the Khokkosh finally arrived. Since the room was dark, the demons were irritated and told Laalkamal to light the lamp. Laalkamal refused, which only served to make the demons angrier.

"What is the name of the prince who is awake?" the Khokkosh demanded.

"Neelkamal is behind and Laalkamal is awake with the sword," Laalkamal responded solemnly.

Hearing the name of Neelkamal and knowing him to be Ajit, the son of the demon queen in a former life, the demons were terrified and crouched back in fear. Feeling a bit skeptical, the Khokkosh then asked to see the tips of Neelkamal's fingernails. Laalkamal took Neelkamal's crown and held it up behind the royal sword so that dreadful shadows of great claws were seen upon the wall.

The Khokkosh shuddered in fear from the other side of the room, thinking that if Neelkamal's fingernails were so big, he must be truly gigantic and dreadful to behold! Yet, they were still not satisfied and asked to see Neelkamal's saliva.

Laalkamal responded by taking some boiling-hot lamp oil and hurling it at the Khokkosh, which burned their thick hair and caused them to flee, shrieking in pain and terror.

After they recovered, the Khokkosh returned and craftily asked to see the prince's tongue. In response, Laalkamal held out the royal sword, and all the demons viciously attacked, thinking that they were seizing the prince's tongue and intending to pull it out of his mouth. Since it was the royal sword, however, the demons' hands were cut and sliced badly, which caused them to lose great quantities of black blood and run away in fear yet again.

A while later, one small demon quietly returned and asked Laalkamal, "Who is awake?"

Forgetting to mention Neelkamal's name first, Laalkamal mistakenly said, "Laalkamal is awake," which roused all of the Khokkosh and caused them to attack him in full force!

"Help me, Neelkamal!" Laalkamal cried out to his sleeping friend.

Awaking from sleep, Neelkamal immediately arose and angrily demanded, "Who dares to fight against me and my mighty sword?"

Neelkamal then attacked the Khokkosh with fury and lit the lamp so that all of the demons were blinded by the flash of light. The powerful prince quickly destroyed all of the Khokkosh and cut them into pieces with his mighty sword.

The two brothers washed their hands because they were soaked with the blood of the Khokkosh. Worn out from the fighting, they immediately lay down and fell into a deep sleep.

The next morning, the king arrived to see the two beautiful princes sleeping peacefully among the dead bodies of the Khokkosh. He was so delighted by what they had successfully done that he gave his kingdom to Neelkamal and Laalkamal and also gave his two beautiful daughters to them in marriage.

In the meantime, the demon queen was hiding out in the human king's palace after paralyzing him and received the news from her two messengers, Ai Rakkhosh and Ki Rakkhosh, that Neelkamal had killed all of the Khokkosh. The demon queen's heart was filled with fear at the news and ordered her two Rakkhosh messengers to change into their human soldier forms and go to the palace of Neelkamal and Laalkamal.

Obediently, the two messengers went to the faraway land and brought the news that the paralyzed King would be restored to full health if the oil of Rakkhosh's head was applied to his body. Immediately, Neelkamal and Laalkamal took their powerful sword and started out on another journey to collect the oil of Rakkhosh's head from the Land of Demons.

Along the journey, Neelkamal and Laalkamal came to a dense forest and took a break under the big Ashwatha Tree. In the tree was a nest of a pair of mythical dragon-like birds that were called Byangoma and Byangomi.

Byangomi said to Byangoma, "Could these be the brave ones who will donate two drops of blood to open the eyes of our offspring?"

Hearing the conversation above them, Neelkamal and Laalkamal agreed to give their blood, so Byangoma collected drops of blood from each of their fingers. As a result, the eyes of the offspring were opened. The whole family was filled with gratitude and one of the young male creatures offered to help the two princes to express his appreciation.

Neelkamal and Laalkamal responded by giving their blessing to all the creatures for a happy life but said that they did not need any help. Two of the male offspring of Byangoma and Byangomi offered to help by flying the two princes on their backs through the sky toward the country of the Rakkhosh and the two princes agreed.

***

After seven days and seven nights of continuous flying, Neelkamal and Laalkamal finally reached a gigantic mountain that stood before their destination. As the morning sun of the eighth day rose in the sky, the two princes surveyed the large field before them, realizing that the Land of Demons was just beyond the horizon.

As they walked forward, Neelkamal collected some seeds of the Kalai Dal and handed them to Laalkamal.

"You must eat these seeds when the Rakkhosh tells you to eat the iron seeds of Kalai Dal."

They continued across the large field and saw tens of thousands of Rakkhosh coming toward them.

Neelkamal shouted, "Grandmother! Grandmother! We have come! I am Neelkamal, your grandson. I am the son of the demon queen. Rakkhosh, welcome me and adore me in your lap!"

The grandmother of the Rakkhosh heard him and said, "Oh, my dear grandson, Neelkamal! Come to me!" As the prince came forward, she adored him in her lap.

The grandmother of the Rakkhosh was named Jatbijti Buri and she smelled like rotting flesh. Neelkamal was irritated by the smell but did not allow it to bother him.

Then Jatbijti Buri looked suspiciously upon Laalkamal and said to Neelkamal, "Grandson, who is this man who smells like a human?"

Neelkamal answered, "He is my brother, Laalkamal."

When Jatbijti Buri still did not believe Neelkamal, she pulled several iron seeds of Kalai Dal from her ugly nose and asked Laalkamal to eat them to prove that he was also a Rakkhosh.

Since Neelkamal had already prepared him, Laalkamal was ready and calmly accepted the iron seeds, switching them with the seeds that Neelkamal had given him and easily eating them. This convinced Jatbijti Buri that Laalkamal was also her grandson, so she took both Neelkamal and Laalkamal in her enormous lap.

As Neelkamal and Laalkamal remained with the Rakkhosh, they could see that the Land of Demons was so vast and dangerous that the only thing it could be compared to was Hell itself. Tens of thousands of demons filled the land with humans and animals so that they always had the flesh of dead bodies to eat. They regularly went out around the world to destroy thousands of human cities and towns, bringing back dead bodies and causing the rotten smell of corpses to fill the whole land.

Whenever the Rakkhosh put Neelkamal and Laalkamal on their backs and flew them around the Land of Demons, the two princes watched all of the terrible scenes take place below them. Neelkamal was convinced that he must do something to protect the human race so that it would not be completely destroyed by all of the horrible demons!

Soon, Neelkamal found a golden opportunity when all of the Rakkhosh went for their weekly haunting of the human countries, far away across the Seven Seas. On that day, Neelkamal and Laalkamal were all alone in the city of the Rakkhosh—not a single demon remained behind!

The two princes walked toward a secret well that was situated on the extreme north side of the Land of Demons. As they reached the well, Neelkamal jumped down inside of it and found a great sword and a golden box, which contained the main lifeline for all of the Rakkhosh, including the demon queen.

As he came back out of the well, Neelkamal opened the golden box and found that two bees were inside. The first bee was Jiyankathi, the lifeline of all of the Rakkhosh. The second bee was Marankathi, the lifeline of the demon queen. Neelkamal took Jiyankathi in his hand and Laalkamal took Marankathi in his.

When the two princes took the two bees in their hands, all of the Rakkhosh felt intense pain! As Neelkamal continued to hold Jiyankathi, the demons throughout the world began to return to their land to save their lifeline. Meanwhile, as Laalkamal held Marankathi, the demon queen became unconscious back in the palace of the paralyzed king.

The Rakkhosh were desperate to prevent the impending danger to their entire Kingdom, so they gathered together to attack Neelkamal as he continued to hold their bee in his hand. Seeing all of the demons coming at him with full force, Neelkamal cut off the two main legs of Jiyankathi, which caused all of the legs of the demon forces to immediately be amputated from their bodies!

Not about to give up, the Rakkhosh continued moving toward Neelkamal, crawling forward with their hands and arms. Neelkamal responded by cutting off the remaining four legs of the bee, which destroyed all of the arms and hands of the demons.

Finally, Neelkamal cut off the head of Jiyankathi, which caused all of the heads of the Rakkhosh to fall to the ground, including the head of Jatbijti Buri. All of the demons were now dead!

After successfully destroying all of the Rakkhosh, Neelkamal and Laalkamal wrapped up the head of Jatbijti Buri with a cloth and put Marankathi back into the golden box. It was time to return to their kingdom, so the two princes summoned the two Byangomi to fly them back across the country.

*** * ***

After three long months and thirteen days of being away from their kingdom, Neelkamal and Laalkamal returned as conquering heroes who successfully overcame the demons. They sent the head of Jatbijti Buri to the kingdom of the demon queen by the two Rakkhosh who were still disguised as human soldiers.

When the demon queen received the dreadful package and saw what it was, she flew into a rage. Feeling desperate, she immediately traveled to the kingdom of Neelkamal and Laalkamal with the intent of attacking the two princes.

As soon as the demon queen arrived, however, Laalkamal took the Marankathi Bee from its golden box, which immediately caused her to fall down and become unconscious. Then Laalkamal killed the bee, which resulted in the demon queen's instantaneous death. The two princes

39

ordered their soldiers to dispose of the horrible, mutilated corpse of the demon queen, and her evil spell was lifted from the whole world.

Immediately afterward, the king and father of the two princes, Ajit and Kushum, recovered from his evil disease. All the people who had deserted the land when the Rakkhosh had killed the two boys also returned to their country. The whole kingdom was full of rejoicing, but they began to search for their beloved princes, Ajit and Kushum.

On the day of celebration, Neelkamal and Laalkamal arrived at the king's country and bowed down to their father, touching his feet with respect and love.

The king was very moved and asked, "Are you my sons, Ajit and Kushum?"

Neelkamal and Laalkamal responded, "We are the reincarnated forms of Ajit and Kushum."

The king was overjoyed and the whole kingdom was full of celebration! After that, the two kingdoms merged. Laalkamal with his wife, Leelaboti, and Neelkamal with his wife, Elaboti, reigned as kings and queens beside their father the king with joy and happiness forever.

The End.

Glossary

Bengali names and phrases from
The Adventure of Neelkamal and Laalkamal

Ajit: The name of the prince who later became Neelkamal.

Byangoma or *Byangomi*: Legendary human-faced birds of Bengali folklore who are portrayed as wise, fortune-telling birds that help the deserving.

Elaboti (or *Ilavati*): The name of the princess married to Neelkamal.

Jatbijti Buri: An old lady without an identity. The demon mother to the demon queen and the demon grandmother of Neelkamal.

Jiyankathi: The bee whose name means Life Stick.

Khokkosh: A smaller type of demon.

Kushum: The inner yellow part of an egg. It is a uni-gender name in the Indian subcontinent and the name of the prince who later became Laalkamal.

Laalkamal: The reincarnated Prince Kushum, son of the King and the human Queen, half-brother to Neel. His name means Red Flower (*Laal*: Red and *Kamal*: Flower).

Leelaboti (or *Lilavati*): The name of the princess married to Laalkamal.

Marankathi: The bee whose name means Death Stick.

Neelkamal: The reincarnated Prince Ajit, son of the King and the Demon Queen, half-brother to Laal. His name means Blue Flower (*Neel*: Blue and *Kamal*: Flower).

Rakkhosh: A bigger kind of demon.

Seeds of Kalai Dal: A type of lentil.

References

Ahmed, W. (2006). *Folk Literature: Banglapedia.*
http://www.banglapedia.org/HT/F_0123.HTM.

Balkin, J.M. (1996). *Deconstruction.* Yale L.J. 743.

Benton, M. (1989). *The Comic Book in America: An Illustrated History.*
Taylor Publishing Company.

Bhatia, T. K. (2006). "Super-Heroes to Super Languages: American
Popular Culture through South Asian Language Comics." *World
Englishes*, 25(2), 279-298. http://doi:10.1111/j.0083-2919.2006.00465.

Burton, T., Director (1989). Movie. *Batman.* USA.

Campbell, J. (1968). *The Hero with a Thousand Faces.* Princeton, N.J.
Princeton University Press.

Coogan, P. (2006). *Superhero: The Secret Origin of a Genre.* A
MonkeyBrain Books Publication. Austin, TX.

Cosentino, D. J. (1998). *African Oral Narrative Traditions: Teaching
Oral Traditions.* New York: Modern Language Association, pp. 174–
188.

Davis, L.C. (2009). *Railing Opinion: Batman, Bernini and Young
Romantics.* The Brooklyn Rail.
http://www.brooklynrail.org/2009/12/artseen/railing-opinion-batman-
bernini-and-young-romantics.

Derrida, J. (1976). *Of Grammatology.* Johns Hopkins Univ. Press.

Dozier, W., Creator (1966-68). Television Series. *Batman.* USA.

Edwardson, R. (2003). "The Many Lives of Captain Canuck: Nationalism, Culture, and the Creation of a Canadian Comic Book Superhero." *Journal of Popular Culture*, 37(2), 184-201. http://doi:10.1111/1540-5931.00063.

Jung, C. G. & Hull, R. F. C. (1981). *The Archetypes and the Collective Unconscious, Collected Works of C.G. Jung,* Vol 9, Part 1. Princeton, N.J.: Princeton University Press.

Lam, P. E. (2007). *Japan's Quest for "Soft Power": Attraction and Limitation.* Springer Science & Business Media.

Nolan, C., Director (2005). Movie. *Batman Begins*. UK. USA.

Nolan, C., Director (2008). Movie. *The Dark Knight*. UK. USA.

Nolan, C., Director (2012). Movie. *The Dark Knight Rises*. UK. USA.

Plouffe, V. (2000). *Deconstructing Batman.* www.architecture.uwaterloo.ca/faculty_projects/terri/.../Batman.

Postrel, V. (2006). "Superhero Worship." *Atlantic Monthly*, 298(3), 140-144.

Ruzicka, J. G. (2010). "American Superheroes and the Politics of Good and Evil." *New Presence: The Prague Journal of Central European Affairs*, 12(2), 46-48.

Shahed, S. (1993). "Bengali Folk Rhymes: An Introduction." *Asian Folklore Studies*, 52(1), 143.

Siddiqui, A. (1980). *Bengali Folklore Collections and Studies: 1800-1947.* Bangla Academy, Dhaka.

Smith, S., Writer (2008). Documentary. *Batman Unmasked*. USA.

Smuts, A. (2008). "The Desire-Frustration Theory of Suspense." *Journal of Aesthetics and Art Criticism*, 66(3), 281-290.

Stabile, C. A. (2009). "Sweetheart, This Ain't Gender Studies: Sexism and Superheroes." *Communication & Critical/Cultural Studies*, 6(1), 86-92.

Steele, R. S. & Swinney, S.V. (1978). "Zane Grey, Carl Jung and the Journey of the Hero." *Journal Of Analytical Psychology*, 23(1), 63-89.

Walker, B. G. (1983). *The Woman's Encyclopedia of Myths and Secrets.* San Francisco: Harper & Row, Publishers.

Williams, K. D. (2011). *Evolution of the Television Superheroes: Comparing Super Friends and Justice League in Terms of Foreign Relation.*